T0380819

CHOOSING OUR FUTURE

Annette Weinerman

WestBow Press books may be ordered through booksellers or by contacting:

WestBow Press
A Division of Thomas Nelson & Zondervan
1663 Liberty Drive
Bloomington, IN 47403
www.westbowpress.com
844.714.3454

ISBN: 978-1-6642-0242-9 (sc)
ISBN: 978-1-6642-0243-6 (e)

Library of Congress Control Number: 2020915706

Print information available on the last page.

WestBow Press rev. date: 02/05/2021

WESTBOW
PRESS®
A DIVISION OF THOMAS NELSON
& ZONDERVAN

Contents

Introduction

My purpose in writing this book is to create a guide that you, the reader, can use to thoughtfully work through a group of topics which are critical to developing a mature, stable life approach.

Each topic is highly personal and complex in nature. It is tempting to skim lightly over such topics and concepts. To dwell on them we must be willing to look under the surface of our everyday behaviors. Most of us would rather not. Yet that is where we discover our heart, our personal truths, our hurts, the lies we've been told and the lies we tell ourselves. It is where we discover all the things that have taken root in our souls which need cleaning out. It is also where we discover the shining beauty of who we are and who we can be.

Choosing Our Future is an invitation to explore the inner workings of your deepest self. It is laid out with three basic components to each topic:

- ➤ One page of highly focused topic content, constructed to probe
  - ♦ What is it?
  - ♦ Why does it matter?
  - ♦ What can we do about it?
- ➤ An illustration, which gives the reader a visual and emotional resting place as they consider the topic
- ➤ A questions section, to help the reader probe and explore their own perspective, reactions, experiences, and beliefs on the topic

It is my hope that you will take the time to think and explore; that you will use the blank lines in the questions sections to write out your thoughts; that this exploration will pique your curiosity to learn and explore more deeply on the topics that touch you. I hope you discover areas where you hunger to know more than this little guide offers; that you feel compelled to look further and deeper. Most of all, I hope you find the path to the future that you want to choose for yourself.

Our Choices

Our lives are an accumulation of the choices we make. Those choices create a path for us – one that stretches behind, enabling us to see the journey we have created, and stretching ahead a bit into the foggy mist of future choices. Fortunately, if we discover our path is not leading to our heart's desires, we can change our choices and create a new path, leading to a different journey.

But changing how we make choices is hard and carries unknown danger. How can we be sure our future choices will lead us to the path we desire? How do we lay a course through the maze of life's choices, opportunities, and possibilities? The answers are really determined by our character. Our strengths and weaknesses drive our choices. The more intentional we can be about anchoring our choices in a clear understanding of sound character, the better our chance to create both a journey and an outcome that truly delights our soul.

This book introduces the choices we must all consider as we seek to know ourselves. It probes the values that establish our character, defining our choices, our behaviors, and our future.

We take such a courageous step because we believe something better will come of the action. It requires that we know ourselves and know our values – that we are convicted of their importance. We do not arrive at such convictions accidentally - we must engage in some exploratory internal work. We must discover what really matters to each of us, personally. Through this exploration, we can achieve the goals of defining our values and establishing our convictions. They become the foundation of our daily behaviors. They enable our courage, creating the change we need through choices large and small.

Are you ready to start exploring yourself? Grab a pen and make some time for yourself, so that you can answer the questions that speak to your heart.

From Wounded to Whole

We are all a bit wounded – some more than others. We often see ourselves as victims, but at times we are also aggressors. Some of us have unhealthy dependencies and some of us are co-dependent. But no matter who we are, we make better choices once we begin a journey to heal the wounded places in our souls. The search for wholeness is a lifetime journey that doesn't end. But it is one well worth making.

To make enough progress that we can look back and say "See how far I have come" often takes many years. And yet if we do not begin, it is like standing in the midst of a fire, afraid to move for fear it will hurt. The truth is, we are already in pain. So, it hurts to stay, and it hurts to move forward. But if we move, we eventually come out on the other side of the fire, where there are new choices and opportunities – what a glorious feeling! And we have learned how to grow and change as we step into our next challenge.

You absolutely will come to a better place if you seek growth. It may feel very uncomfortable for you and everyone around you, as you change. Change alters the balance in relationships and the known expectations. For everyone involved, even unreasonable expectations that are known and understood can feel better than the uncertainty of new expectations. These are growing pains that are well worth the effort.

This is a journey that you don't have to make alone. There is an enormous amount of excellent information available - guidebooks, counsellors, and support groups to help you find your way. All of the topics introduced here are key concepts that you will need to evaluate on your journey. Some topics you will pass through easily. For other topics you will need to dig deep, examining parts of yourself that you didn't know existed, searching out all the support resources you can find. You will know what you need, if you listen to yourself honestly.

What are your deepest wounds?

_____

_____

_____

_____

_____

Which wound / hurt are you most afraid of confronting? Why?

_____

_____

_____

_____

_____

Which wound has caused you the most emotional damage? Why?

_____

_____

_____

_____

Why do you want to heal?

_____

_____

_____

_____

Our Journey

Being human is a marvelous and difficult journey. We are born into and encounter circumstances in life that by definition are beyond our control and not of our choosing. They trigger core emotions that are fundamental elements of our humanity. How we manage our emotions, choose to respond in those situations, and what we learn creates the story of our lives.

All too often we awake somewhere along our journey and realize that although we have been pushing and pulling on our oars as hard as we know how, our ship is adrift. Perhaps we are not sure where we are headed. Maybe we are not sure we know how to get where we want to go. Or most terribly, we discover our destination is not really the utopia we expected….we have put tremendous effort into seeking something that does not deliver our dreams.

How do we make choices in life that land us on the golden shores of a joyous life, where we leave a lasting legacy for those who come behind us? Without a meaningful vision and map to guide our path, how can we arrive at the life that we long for?

Can you imagine how your life will unfold? Does your vision include making a difference? What will people say about your character and personality? How do you know you are on the right path to reach your vision? When you are gone, will you be legendary, with inspiring stories that people love to share? Will you leave footprints that others aspire to walk in? What will be your legacy?

Each person's self-exploration, choices and journey are unique. Yet we share common challenges, especially in dealing with our emotions. Controlling our emotional responses is one of the important ways we have control in life. It is our best tool for fighting our personal inferno, finding our way to the other side and building the life we long for.

How is your life today different than you expected it to be?

_____

_____

_____

_____

_____

What different choices would have changed your journey? How?

_____

_____

_____

_____

_____

What does your ideal vision for your future life look like?

_____

_____

_____

_____

What do you think you will need to do to achieve your vision?

_____

_____

_____

_____

Trusting Our Highest Power

We are both physical and spiritual beings. Our spiritual element is as real as the physical. How many times have you felt the emotion in the room, without anyone speaking a word? Known someone's unexpressed thoughts? Longed for peace and rest for your soul? This intangible part of us, which extends beyond our intellect, is deeply connected to our emotions and our sense of self.

Most of us have been exposed to the concept of a higher power; an omnipotent, omniscient, omnipresent creator that intends good for us. We know "Him" by different names: God, Allah, Yahweh, Higher Power. For this book, we will refer to this concept as our Highest Power. We may even accept His existence, reasoning that the spiritual elements of our humanity must come from somewhere outside the physical realm. However, to trust this Being with our future? It is a concept that we struggle with and resist because it threatens our very sense of self and independence.

Certainly, in the midst of life's agonizing moments, our first reaction is to say "Of course, I cannot trust Him with my future…look what He has allowed in my life so far." In truth, if we confront the facts of our life and this world honestly, He is not the author of our sufferings. We bring them upon ourselves, and we cannot rely upon our own strength or wisdom to deliver us. Facing this necessary truth opens the door for us to trust Him. It can be one of the hardest challenges we ever face. It is the first, most important step in mastering emotions and making better choices – accepting that there is a resource greater than ourselves that we can turn to in times of emotional difficulty.

We may struggle with and question the concept of acknowledging and trusting a Highest Power. We may wonder and ponder on it all our lives. But we must hold onto it, even in the midst of our doubt. Without it, we drift unsure and often overwhelmed, doubting our purpose and our value. Life is often bigger than we are. In those moments, the greatest gift we can give ourselves is the acceptance of a loving, generous, and merciful power whom we can trust, because He has a purpose for us beyond this present moment.

What were you taught about God, Allah, Yahweh, or a Higher Power?

_____

_____

_____

_____

How did that teaching affect your emotions and your choices?

_____

_____

_____

_____

What do you believe is true, today?

_____

_____

_____

_____

_____

How would trusting a Highest Power now change your world view?

_____

_____

_____

_____

Our Character

To go forward from where we are, we must take a look at the foundation for our character – a foundation that will enable us to manage our emotions and make wise choices. We must establish the internal values that will lead us to our goals. Like everything else, this requires some soul searching.

What is most important to you? Enduring love relationships? Financial security and material comfort? Inner peace? Joy of life? We all have a list of things we would sacrifice all else to achieve. And yet, the only thing that endures, ever-present in all our circumstances, impacting every choice and transcending this lifetime, is our character. Character is formed through the repeated practice of our values. It becomes incredibly important to our future to base our values on enduring principles of goodness and live by those principles with rigorous integrity.

Perhaps more than any other virtue, integrity requires courage. Courage to do the right thing, even at personal cost. It is so tempting to succumb to the seduction of the convenient choice. Courage gives integrity its strength. Without it, our convictions are just a nice set of platitudes. With the courage to act, those same convictions become integrity - value based choices we make and live by every day.

Integrity requires courage, but it walks best with humility. If we take a stand on a matter, but do so with arrogance, we lack the compassion needed to treat others with respect, especially those who choose differently. We are closed to other perspectives that enrich our insight and understanding. More harm than good comes from arrogant integrity.

Humble integrity is gentle and kind. It models the way, making the path to good choices clear. It inspires and encourages others and brings confident peace. It enables us to "protect and serve" in the best possible way. How do you display courage, humility, and integrity in your daily life? How do you make these a deeper part of your character? Let's look at the underlying elements that affect our character in the remaining pages.

How would you define character? What are the key elements of good character?

_____

_____

_____

_____

What would be on your prioritized list of things that are most important?

_____

_____

_____

_____

How would you achieve your goals, while practicing good character?

_____

_____

_____

_____

_____

How does practicing integrity make it easier / harder to achieve your goals?

_____

_____

_____

_____

_____

Respect and Trust

Respect, trust, and love are three of our deepest psychological needs and are often spoken of interchangeably. But they are not the same. Each one meets a different core need, exposes a different vulnerability, and is enacted differently.

We hunger so much for respect that we think it must be a right that we can demand or a reward that we can earn. Is there a specific set of behaviors that earn respect, or does it seem like an endless pursuit? In truth, no matter who you are or how you behave, respect is extended to you by others.

While there are behaviors that command respect, not everyone is able to give it. Respect is like a blanket that offers courtesy and kindness in all circumstances. Some of us do not have this blanket even for ourselves, or it is so small that we do not have it to share with others. Some of us have a large thin blanket, easily torn. A few have a large, warm, embracing blanket that is shared with all. Respect is an ongoing choice we make in how we deal with others. It does not require reciprocation. It is not dependent on the depth or duration of the relationship. We offer it by being consciously courteous in our tone, our words and our impact on others. How big is your respect blanket?

Conversely, trust is a deliberate choice to make ourselves vulnerable. At the beginning of a relationship we extend limited trust, based on our assessment of the others' character - their trustworthiness. We then unconsciously probe every word and action for the risk associated with giving our ongoing trust. As we inevitably experience broken trust in life, we find it harder to trust and we raise our protective barriers. We become isolated souls, hungry for connection. If we venture into relationships where trust, vulnerability and giving are not required, we falsely imagine that we are maintaining emotional safety. In actuality, we are creating empty relationships that invite further betrayal. Where are your trust barriers? Have you emotionally isolated yourself to stay "safe"? Setting appropriate boundaries and holding to them, for ourselves and others, can help us risk trusting and enable us to be trustworthy. Give respect, extend trust, and be trustworthy to lay a foundation for loving others.

What is your strongest area of distrust: What is the underlying cause for it?

_____

_____

_____

_____

What areas of trust do you value highly? Why?

_____

_____

_____

_____

What can you trust about your Highest Power?

_____

_____

_____

_____

What do you think healthy trust would look like in your primary relationships?

_____

_____

_____

_____

Unconditional Love

There are many definitions for love...giving, sharing, sacrifice, a choice. It brings us exquisitely close and forges the deepest connections. Unconditional love is the pinnacle of loving behavior. It is the surrender of self to the needs of another, while expecting nothing in return. How terrifying! How do we give unconditional love without losing ourselves? The risk seems great. And indeed, it is.

Giving love threatens our deeply held need for independence. Even in a relatively whole relationship the need for independence is often deeper than the need for love and connection. When we are forced to choose, our natural choice is survival of self - independence over love and connection. And so, we unwittingly drive wedges of disconnection into the relationships we hold dear. Ultimately, we lose out on life's most precious gift.

Is your love built on a foundation of trust and respect? Do you attach conditions to your love? What do you need, for love to thrive? How do you heal broken trust, so that your love can survive?

One of the best tools for a close relationship is communicating. That means listening with understanding, not just talking. It means being candid and making ourselves vulnerable. What fears make that hard for you to do? Practice intentionally repeating back to someone what you think they just said. Did you learn something new? Does it help clarify? Is there a point at which your communication routinely breaks down? Do you know the triggers? Are you willing to discuss them with each other?

In a loving and enduring relationship, we treasure another, placing the other's needs for emotional security above our own. When we surround this love with respect and trust, we support our loved ones in the freedom to be themselves. The security and strength this adds to our love relationships is immeasurable. The sacrifice we make by joyfully putting others first has its own reward. You will gain more than you give!

How do you express love for those who are precious to you?

_____

_____

_____

_____

_____

What conditions do you attach to your love?

_____

_____

_____

_____

What would you need, to be able to love someone who has betrayed you?

_____

_____

_____

_____

What is sacrificial love for you? At what point does it raise resentment?

_____

_____

_____

_____

Tough Love

Almost all of us have been involved with or know someone who struggles with some type of unhealthy dependency. One of life's biggest challenges is finding ourselves in a relationship where we love someone but must draw boundaries and refuse to accept destructive behavior. If we violate the integrity of our value-based boundaries in order to keep the relationship, we are enabling their self-destructive behavior and failing to be true to our values. We are not truly loving them or ourselves. This path is guaranteed to yield a broken relationship. Alternatively, if we stand by our values, and communicate our ongoing love for them, the relationship may feel broken, but we leave the door open and give the relationship a chance to heal in the future.

This "tough love" is a painful but at times necessary path to walk. It is so tough because it is a conscious choice to make value-based decisions that place integrity over the immediate demands of the other person. It requires us to take a clear-eyed look at the relationship, asking if those demands are true needs, or just wants? Are the wants self-serving – for either ourselves or the other person? What will be the long-term consequence of meeting those wants? Is it a spiritual, emotional, physical or financial price that we are willing to pay? Is the price appropriate? Will it hurt others who are peripherally involved? Are there others who need to be protected? The honest answers to these difficult questions are how we count the cost of loving a broken person and determine our own boundaries. Every person is different in what they are able to give in these situations, and there is no right or wrong response.

One thing is certain however…even as we set appropriate boundaries and give what we are able, we must accept that we do not control the outcome. There is a moment for letting go, for turning the results over to our Highest Power, for knowing that no matter how much we love the person, we may not be the one who saves them.

Tough love is not just taking a tough stance toward someone we love. Tough love is tough on us. It is hard to do, because it hurts. Our heart longs to meet their every desire, and yet that may not be for the best. Instead we make the hard choices and take the hard stand because it is our best expression of unconditional love.

What boundaries are important for you, to maintain your sense of self?

_____

_____

_____

_____

What price are you willing to pay to retain your "tough love" relationship?

_____

_____

_____

_____

What is the hardest value or boundary for you to stand by? Why is that?

_____

_____

_____

_____

What do you envision this relationship would look like if it were healthy?

_____

_____

_____

_____

Self-Control and Letting Go

The concept of letting go is an especially hard one for most of us. We only let go when our fingers are pried loose, one-by-one. The more uncertain the world feels, the more we trust no other and want to control our outcomes. However, the more tightly we hold onto something, the more likely it is to slip from our grasp. Our gasp of horror and attempt to catch it as it falls are all in vain.

Does this mean we should never try to plan or influence anything? Of course not! But it does mean we go into situations knowing that things may change. Most importantly, we let go of our certainty that we know best. We embrace other's concerns, respect their boundaries, and weigh their needs in our plans.

Self-Control is the flip side of the control coin. It is controlling our own responses. This can only be done by letting go of the desire to control external situations or the behaviors of others. We must ask ourselves and answer honestly: What are we really attempting to achieve through controlling behavior? Is our way always best? What about those terrible times when circumstances or other people are radically damaging to us and ours?

Where do we find the self-control to let go when it feels so frightening? Accept the reality of the situation and lean into our Highest Power as a source to guide our response and strengthen our self-control. In every circumstance we can seek out the guidance of our Highest Power through meditation, prayer, and reading in order to find our most positive response and do our best to act on it.

When we use self-control to let go, we release the frustration and regret that comes from attempting to mold the world to our will. We can also avoid the high price of damaged relationships, which is an inevitable outcome of attempting to control others. Instead, we discover that new and unexpected possibilities present themselves and better choices become possible.

What is particularly hard for you to let go of in a relationship? Why is that?

_____

_____

_____

_____

What does self-control mean for you in a relationship?

_____

_____

_____

_____

What areas of a relationship are hard for you to practice self-control?

_____

_____

_____

_____

What does the balance between letting go and self-control look like for you?

_____

_____

_____

_____

Anger, Hate, and Fear Illuminated

A powerful force, anger sometimes feels good or right in the moment, but the long-term consequences are never really positive. Hate is anger's monster child, sustained and nurtured by deep resentment. While hate's flames may flicker and dance around the feet of its recipient, it consumes the souls of those who harbor it. These emotions are enemies that must be released to die. It requires great courage to confront the underlying causes of our anger and hate. So, where to begin? We have to understand the source.

First, know that anger is a secondary emotion - something triggers the anger. Anger and hate are not independent, self-initiated, self-sustaining emotions. They are the visceral surface manifestations of something much deeper. The "something deeper" is almost always fear. Fear of failure, fear of ridicule or disrespect, fear of weakness or another person's power over our life, or fear of loss. Fear is the true destructive beast. It destroys our soul long before we damage someone else with our rage or hate.

Fear paralyzes. When gripped by fear, we cannot find our way forward. It often keeps us from taking bold or courageous action to solve our problems. How then do we master fear? It is a long arduous journey to unearth and denounce the lies we have been told and believed. Those lies are the root of our fears. To separate truth from lies requires a careful review of the ideas we accept about ourselves and our world. Spend some time journaling about what you believe, what really drives you, and why. How much of it is based in fact versus someone else's perspective? How balanced are their views and why should you accept them? As you tear down your fears, what is your new world view? What new truths will replace your fears?

Fears are like the dark shadows on the wall in our childhood room at night. They loom large and frightening, until the light of truth is turned on, and then phff...they vanish! Sometimes turning the light on is a simple flip of the switch - a moment of illumination. Sometimes it is the lighting of one candle after another - learning and repeating a truth to combat the lies, until our hearts can truly embrace and accept the strength buried under the fear. It is a journey that we all need to make, to be free of fear and its dark companions, anger, and hate.

What are your deepest sources of anger?

_____

_____

_____

_____

What are key triggers for your anger? Why are they triggers?

_____

_____

_____

_____

What are your biggest fears? How are they linked to your anger triggers?

_____

_____

_____

_____

If you could eliminate your biggest fears, how would your life be different?

_____

_____

_____

_____

Self-Justification and Blaming

We use self-justification and blaming to rationalize our failures internally (self-justification) and externally (blaming). They are among the most universal practices in the arsenal of human self-defense. Our sanity depends on our ability to reconcile our beliefs and our behaviors. As a result, we constantly seek to rationalize our actions to our value system. If they don't align well in a particular situation, the easiest solution is to make an excuse or blame someone else. If what we are doing is some-one else's fault, we don't need to change. They do!

In reality, self-justification and blaming are delay tactics at best…we use them to avoid important moments of truth when we need to own our choices and their consequences. Sometimes we firmly hold onto these tactics for years. Over time, it becomes harder and harder to be honest with ourselves. Unfortunately, our inability to own our choices feeds other destructive emotions, like sustained resentment, unforgiving anger, and ongoing self-indulgence.

To be on the receiving end of blame can be even more damaging. As we internalize the blaming that may constantly bombard us, we become defeated, losing belief in ourselves and our capabilities. We may even go so far as to begin blaming ourselves for someone else's behavior. It becomes an endless downward spiral. If we cannot identify blaming attacks and set boundaries around how we are treated, then we are easily destroyed.

Since it has such a powerful impact, we need to tackle this damaging habit. Self-justification often starts with "well actually…" or "I was just…". Blaming generally starts with "you" or someone-else's name and can be accompanied by feelings of righteous indignation. These words and emotions are clues that this tricky habit is in play. To rid yourself of this behavior requires brutal self-honesty and constant vigilance. Stop to dig deeper when you recognize it is happening.

Releasing self-justification and blame can give you big AHA! moments that are pivotal to making different choices, leading to the life you seek.

What self-justification have you been holding onto?

_____

_____

_____

_____

Who have you been hurting with your blaming?

_____

_____

_____

_____

What habit are you afraid to confront, frequently prompting you to blame?

_____

_____

_____

_____

What blame have you accepted inappropriately?

_____

_____

_____

_____

Forgiveness

Injustice, real or perceived in one form or another, is the source of most resentment, bitterness, and hate. Resentment over past injustice feeds hate and anger, keeping it alive. Fear of continued injustice causes us to double down on our anger. We do not see that the hate shackles us, that our souls are broken by bitterness and anger. These negative emotions are more destructive than the injustice, disrespect or cruelty that hurt us. We allow that person or event great power over us when we are so consumed. There is only one path to freedom from these tyrants...Release the need for justice, retribution, and vengeance through forgiveness. But how?

First, we must forgive ourselves for our shortfalls and failures. Why is this important? If we cannot forgive ourselves by accepting our own humanity, how can we do the same for others? Whether it is respect, love, or forgiveness for others, we must give ourselves the same gift first. We must see ourselves as worthy, before we can see others as worthy. Forgiveness is integral to healing, for ourselves and for those we need to forgive.

How do we forgive ourselves and others? Consider that expectations of perfection, while admirable, are false. In truth, we all fail miserably in very important ways. We know it and our souls hunger for redemption. It is one of the unexplainable mysteries that lead us to seek a Highest Power, hoping and then believing that forgiveness is possible. Humbling ourselves to ask for that forgiveness once again brings us into conflict with our need for independence. And yet, we cannot find peace or see ourselves as worthy without the redemption of divine forgiveness.

Once we accept forgiveness, we must take action to change our own behavior. Focus on controlling ourselves, rather than others. Pray for those we must forgive. Leave justice to our Highest Power. Trust Him for an ultimate balancing of the scales. Yes, we have a great desire for vengeance at times. We want to be the hand of justice. However, it is our very tendency to human error that mandates we leave retribution in the hands of our Highest Power. Be grateful for grace and mercy, freely given. Have no doubt that we all stand before His justice and are found wanting, and then forgiven. Treat forgiveness as a most precious gift, both when you receive and when you give it.

What were you taught about forgiveness? What does it mean to you now?

_____

_____

_____

_____

What role does your Highest Power play in forgiveness?

_____

_____

_____

_____

What are the benefits to you if you forgive others for deep wounds?

_____

_____

_____

_____

How will you release your need for justice, retribution, and vengeance?

_____

_____

_____

_____

Mercy and Grace

Mercy and grace are often spoken of together. What links them? They are opposite ends of the same spectrum.... where unexpected gifts are generously bestowed.

In mercy we do not receive the consequences that we deserve – an unmerited pardon. In grace we receive benefits we do not earn – an abundance of blessings. Grace follows mercy, just as kindness follows forgiveness. Mercy sets us free. Grace leads us to abiding joy and hope.

Mercy is central to both forgiveness and hope. Forgiveness accepts a failure and moves beyond it. While our failures and wrong doing may have inherent consequences, mercy removes the deserved penalty. The difference between consequences and penalties is an important distinction to note: consequences are the natural result of an action, while a penalty is a price that is imposed to deliver justice. When we receive mercy, the price for justice is removed and forgiven. Although the inherent consequences may remain, we do not have to bear the burden of a penalty. A better future becomes possible.

If we cannot accept the gift of mercy, then life feels hopeless. If we cannot find the generosity to extend mercy to others, then we isolate ourselves in anger and self-righteous judgement. Giving and receiving grace - unconditional, undeserved goodness - opens our hearts to all the good that is possible and encourages us to hope for the future. What can you hope for differently if you accept forgiveness? What relationship would you be able to change if you offered mercy? How can you bestow grace on someone?

Passing these gifts on to others feels good. But like everything else we have discussed; it is only possible if we have first allowed ourselves to receive mercy and grace from our Highest Power. Mercy and grace are truly the light at the end of the tunnel.

What have you been taught about grace and mercy?

_____

_____

_____

_____

What do you believe now about grace and mercy?

_____

_____

_____

_____

Have you ever received mercy or grace from anyone? Given it?

_____

_____

_____

_____

How do you need to see yourself differently, to believe you are worthy?

_____

_____

_____

_____

From Grief to Hope

An abiding sense of loss or sadness for all that is lost or could have been...grief comes to all of us sooner or later, and for some it is a constant companion. We need hope to help us maintain our emotional balance.

We grieve about all kinds of losses in life. People who are precious to us, lost innocence, lost opportunity, pain - ours and that of those we love. In fact, there is so much to grieve for that we can get lost in the sadness. Grief is an imprecise process: although there are some broad steps that we go through related to a specific loss, it does not follow a tidy pattern. It comes and goes in waves that sometimes feel like a tsunami. If we have experienced a great deal of loss, it can become part of our outlook. To keep from falling into what feels like a bottomless well, we need something that will help us to look up and out.

We call that something hope. It is as essential to the survival of our souls as water is to our bodies. Hope compels us forward when we have no other reason to continue. It inspires us and gives us courage to act. And it enables us to survive our grief...it brings a ray of light to our darkest hours. If we struggle against recurring darkness, it is our sunlight. What are your hopes for the future? Are they only for this life? Do you have an eternal hope? Is there something that inspires you and keeps you going when the odds feel overwhelmingly against you?

We choose what we hope for. It is tied very closely to what we believe. This is so important, because if we don't really believe in our Highest Power, another life beyond this one, and the grace and love available for us, then the only things that we can hope for are the physical things of this life. Indeed, we should hope for our heart's desires in this life - but they are not enough. In our deepest, darkest hours of grief, despair, and even shame, how can our hope be enough if it is not anchored to a mercy, love, and redeeming grace that is greater than we are? We need hope for the future. It gives us a way to let go of all the things that we fear and cannot conquer. We are able to look forward with confidence to how we will be transformed, and we are able to hope for a better tomorrow.

What are some personal sources of recurring grief for you?

_____

_____

_____

_____

What are some sources of recurring hope for you?

_____

_____

_____

_____

What links can you create between your sources of grief and hope?

_____

_____

_____

_____

What hope will you think about to counteract your moments of despair?

_____

_____

_____

_____

Patient Kindness

Kindness is a conscious choice to behave in a generously caring and considerate manner. It is not a dip of the quill used to neatly dot an "i" - a single moment in time, but a broad brush sweepingly applied to all our interactions. Patient kindness ensures the "brush is always loaded with paint" - that we will not run out of kindness as the day goes on. If this sounds saintly, it is. We all fail at times. However, the world is better for our efforts.

For many of us rage, anger, and high levels of frustration are a habit. We discover early in life that a certain level of this behavior is tolerated, and we give ourselves permission to vent at that level. Breaking this habit requires replacing it with something positive. Patience, kindness and compassion are alternate responses that we can choose. Over time they become our new habit.

We all have triggers that instantly take us out of our patient and compassionate mode. What are yours? Does your loss of patience instantly erupt into anger? Do you have some tools that will help you to master such moments? In an instant of frustration, the old classic count to ten, has some legitimate value. It causes your brain to pause and gives you a chance to choose your response. It can be helpful to have a mantra (a short meaningful saying) that you can repeat in moments of frustration to help you gain perspective. Using these types of tools can move our responses from impulsive to intentional and help us change our habits.

The human soul has limited resources to give away in the form of patience, kindness, and compassion. We need to "reload our brush" daily with a fresh supply of these virtues to make them part of our character. We do this by connecting to our Highest Power. Prayer, meditation, and inspirational reading are all good means of daily renewal.

There is a positive energy in the universe that is readily available to us, and it has an awesome synergy when it flows between people in the form of patient kindness.

What resentments keep you from feeling kindness at times?

_____

_____

_____

_____

How are patience and kindness linked for you?

_____

_____

_____

_____

What are some underlying fears behind your triggers for losing patience?

_____

_____

_____

_____

What daily activities will help you to "reload" your patience kindness?

_____

_____

_____

_____

Nurturing Self, Nurturing Family

We have an abiding bond of blood, experience, or faith with those we consider family. Family are life's greatest gift. It is our sacred privilege to protect and nurture our family - something we can only do if we first protect and nurture ourselves. What a paradox! We want to give them all, and yet unless we nurture ourselves, we can become like a well run dry, with nothing left to give.

We believe that we are too busy to make time for ourselves. Our tasks and responsibilities are too important. Others depend on us and we cannot let them down. We rather vainly imagine that our world will stop spinning if we step off for an hour a day and devote ourselves to self-nurturing. In an odd way, it requires strong self-discipline to make time for "me". To become present in the moment with ourselves and the things that bring us peace or joy is no easy task.

We nurture self with experiences that feed and stretch our souls - music, poetry, dance, literature, worship, reflection. We need to include those that are most core in our daily practices, and others as often as possible, so that we have variety in our "soul food". These experiences expand our thinking, add to our wisdom, and energize us to generously share our strength.

What are some of your favorite things to do? Do you enjoy peace and quiet, or are you energized by people and activities? What is your favorite type of music? Listen to some. Your favorite literature? Read it. Your favorite TV show? Watch it. Yoga or meditation brings you peace? Get up 30 minutes early to make the time. Rolling on the floor in silly games with your children? Get down there! Does it feed your soul to cook, paint or craft a beautiful item? Do it!

We are amazingly more successful at all those tasks we imagine are so important once we make time to nurture ourselves. Then we are able to nurture our family by sharing with them all the best of who we are.

What emotional barriers keep you from nurturing yourself?

_____

_____

_____

_____

_____

What are some specific activities that would help you to nurture yourself?

_____

_____

_____

_____

_____

What activities do you believe are more important than self-nurturing?

_____

_____

_____

_____

How will your relationships benefit if you take time to nurture yourself?

_____

_____

_____

_____

Happiness, Gratitude, and Joy

Happiness and joy are another pair of emotions that we speak of interchangeably, which are actually quite distinct.

Happiness occurs when we experience something delightful. It lasts as long as the experience and lingers while we are able to hold onto the memory of our delight. Life should be liberally sprinkled with happy experiences.

Joy is a more abiding emotion. It is able to transcend circumstances because it is rooted in gratitude for the positive fundamentals of our lives. We do not experience the sustaining strength of joy without first coming to a place of gratitude.

Gratitude is our intentional recognition of all that is good in our lives and in the world. It requires taking the time to "count our blessings" and then give thanks for them. How often do you do this? Is there a daily time you can dedicate to gratitude – perhaps that last 5 minutes before you fall asleep or with your first cup of coffee? Joy is a natural outcome of a daily practice of gratitude. It gradually changes our view of life, enabling us to rejoice in all that we treasure.

Peace with Joy! It sounds like the perfect human state. To be at rest in heart and mind, and at the same time bubbling over with gratitude for the wondrous gifts of our lives - what could be better? In truth it is an elusive state. It comes rarely and lasts briefly - a moment, an hour, a day. But as we make choices that help us to grow in gratitude, faith, love, patient kindness, and humility - as these virtues become a deeper part of who we are, so does peace with joy! If the passing of time and gaining maturity have a compensation, this is it.

We will struggle with our fears, our hurts, our doubts, and our very human responses as long as we live. But, by aspiring to courageously live out our heart's truths, we can look forward with hope, and have confidence in our legacy. And therein lies peace with joy!

What are some things that make you happy?

_____

_____

_____

_____

_____

What brings you joy?

_____

_____

_____

_____

Do you believe that you deserve happiness and joy? Why or why not?

_____

_____

_____

_____

What part of your day will you set aside for practicing gratitude?

_____

_____

_____

_____

Choosing Our Future

We have touched on several of the core emotions and concepts that we each must grapple with, in order to make mature choices and create a joyous life. As a final thought, contemplate the lasting impact our choices and our lives have on others. What is our legacy? We can be certain that someone is watching us. What do they see, what will they remember, what will they learn? For better or worse, we are modeling the way for someone, somewhere.

Everyone struggles. We have big wins and make big mistakes right out there where everyone can see them. That doesn't really matter so much. What does matter is how we handle it all. We are modeling the way for those who come behind us. Do we leave footprints they will want to follow?

Do we love unconditionally? Do we risk vulnerability by offering respect and trust? Do we walk with humility and generosity in our success? Do we display courage and integrity when faced with hard choices? Do we forgive and let go of painful wounds? Do we have compassion, patience, and kindness for others? If we have lost our way, are we willing to make a significant course correction?

Perhaps the most important part of modeling the way is that we remain willing to share our journey. When we are willing to share our broken and amazing human story, others can see that we keep going...we do not give up...we keep seeking and growing. Our willingness to be vulnerable, exposing our strengths and weaknesses, our successes and failures, helps others find the path to a flourishing life.

Our future awaits us. Our journeys are created one step at a time - one emotion, one reaction, one choice, one decision at a time. It is an exhilarating and clarifying moment to understand that our choices today shape our opportunities for tomorrow. Every day, we can intentionally choose our path, through our responses to all the joys and challenges that we face. The opportunity for an amazing life stretches out in front of us. So, I ask you - what future do you choose?

What do you want your legacy to be?

_____

_____

_____

_____

_____

What will you need to change in your life to create your legacy?

_____

_____

_____

_____

_____

For whom do you want to model the way and leave a positive legacy?

_____

_____

_____

_____

What will be your next step?

_____

_____

_____

_____

Summary Questions:

How do you envision your future now?

_____

_____

_____

_____

What was the most impactful topic for you?

_____

_____

_____

_____

What will you choose differently in the future?

_____

_____

_____

_____

What is the hardest change to make, to make your new choice happen?

_____

_____

_____

_____

Acknowledgments

This has been a very personal work. Although it does not contain personal stories as such, it still feels very much like my soul laid bare. So, a special thank you to all my early readers, including Crystal Adams, Kristen Bettes, Lew Sharpless, April Smith, and Gregory Thompson, who encouraged me to go forward with this book, and who provided invaluable feedback.

A particular thanks to Debbie Houglum, Charlene Benson, David Bettes, and Dave Russell, who all provided comments and discussion that encouraged me to dig deeper and deliver more.

Thank you to my children and grandchildren for being my inspiration in numerous ways they cannot even imagine. My family are my greatest life treasure and my greatest source of learning and growth.

Regarding the lovely photographs we've shared…all are personal and family photos, taken from our travels and times together.

Special honor belongs to the artist of the cover image, my mother Anne Howard. Although she has been gone since 1987, she sought most earnestly to lay a firm foundation of character and courage in her children, thereby leaving a lasting legacy.

Most of all, thank you to my beloved husband Al, who graciously spent endless hours talking through the concepts with me, helping me clarify my thoughts along the way and patiently reading every change. He is the one who models the way for me.